# Learn
# Backgammon

# in 10
## minutes

**Brian Byfield**

Illustrations by Gray Jolliffe

BATSFORD

First published in the United Kingdom in 2013 by
Batsford, 10 Southcombe Street, London W14 0RA

An imprint of Anova Books Company Ltd

ISBN 978 1 84994 059 7

A CIP catalogue record for this book is available from the
British Library.

20 19 18 17 16 15 14 13
10 9 8 7 6 5 4 3 2 1

Reproduction by Rival Colour Ltd, UK
Printed and bound by 1010 Printing International Ltd, China

## Introduction

Backgammon is a racing game. A race made more exciting because each player will be trying to win the race and, at the same time, to stop and block their opponent. It is a board game of odds and calculations with many twists and turns. A gambling race played with dice for money. You don't have to play for money, but it's more fun if you do.

The objective is to get you playing as quickly as possible. To begin with you don't need to know every single rule, procedure or matter of etiquette – you can learn those as you go along. Right, as we've only got ten minutes, let's get started.

# GETTING
# STARTED

Although backgammon looks complicated, it's an easy game to learn. Fast, fun and a wonderful workout for the brain. Good players skilfully arrange for lady luck to be on their side; top players 'see' the board, both its dangers and its many possibilities.

Backgammon is a game for two players. Each player has 15 checkers, which they move according to the roll of their two dice. The aim of the game is to move all your checkers around and off the board before your opponent. The game is played on a board, which comes in its own box. Hopefully, you have one in front of you.

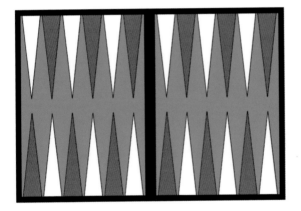

The board has 24 narrow spikes called points.
Their colours alternate to make counting easier.

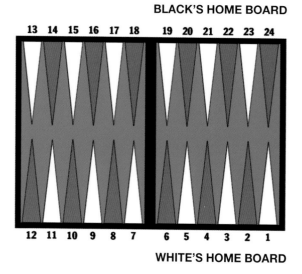

The board is separated by a ridge down the centre called the bar; on the board both players have a home board, and each point is numbered from 1 to 24.

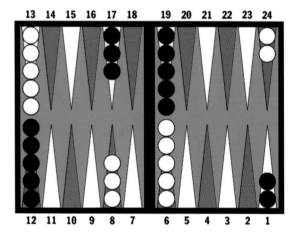

This is how the board is set up to start the game.

Each player's checkers are a mirror image of the other. Each player has five checkers on the 13 point, five checkers on the 6 point, three checkers on the 8 point and two checkers on the 24 point.

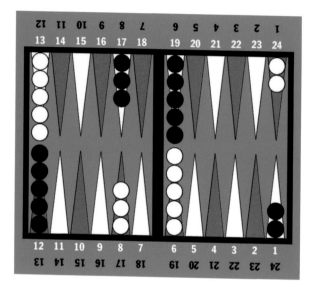

Black's point numbers are inverted, so White's 24 point is his 1 point, and White's 17 point is his 8 point and so on.

Don't worry about Black at the moment, because
we are concentrating on you, and in this book
you will always be playing White.

Each player has a dice cup and two dice.

To decide who goes first, both players throw one of their dice. If they throw the same number, they throw again. The highest throw wins. Let's say, you threw the highest, so you get to go first. You will be White and you will move anti-clockwise into your home board. Black will move clockwise.

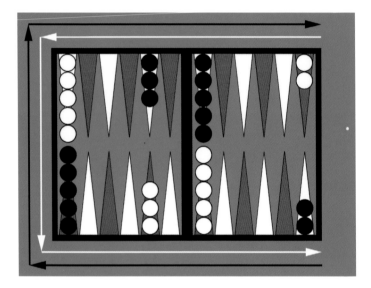

You now move your checkers according to the numbers thrown. For instance, if you had thrown a six and your opponent a four, you can move one checker six points (spaces) and one checker four points. Or you can you move one checker ten points (six plus four).

After that, each player throws both dice and moves their checkers alternately.

Let's say you are playing White and throw a three and a one. If you moved one checker from point 8 to point 5, and another checker from point 6 to point 5, it would be recorded as 8/5 6/5. Your board would now look like this:

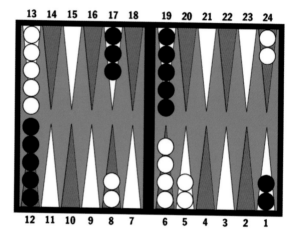

You can move to any open point, any point occupied by your own checkers or any point with one of your opponent's checkers. You cannot land on a point where your opponent has two or more checkers. If you can move to a point where your opponent has one checker only (called a 'blot'), you can knock her checker off the board. This is called 'hitting'.

In the following example, depending on your throw, you can move your white checker to any point in your home board, except 5. You can also hit Black's checker on point 4.

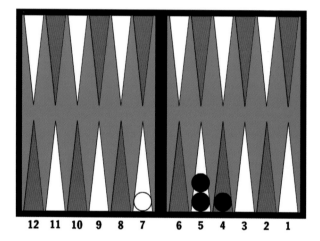

12 11 10 9 8 7 6 5 4 3 2 1

When a player has been hit, her checker is placed on the bar in the centre of the board.

When you hit your opponent's checker, your checker will occupy that point.

A player with a checker or checkers on the bar must move her checkers back on to the board before she can move any others. To get back on to the board the player must throw a number that allows her to occupy a point or hit her opponent. Remember, she cannot land on a point where there is more than one of her opponent's checkers.

## Rolling Doubles

If a player rolls doubles, let's say two sixes, he can move four sixes. If the roll is two and two, it's doubled to four twos, and so on.

## Hit and Run

If you hit your opponent's checker, you are allowed to run for safety.

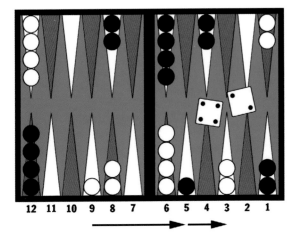

In the example above, let's say White rolls a four and a two. He can hit Black's checker on the 5 point with his checker from the 9 point, then move on to the safety of his 3 point. Black now has to go to the bar.

## Bearing Off

When a player has moved all his checkers into his home board, he can start to 'bear off'.

For instance, if you roll a six and a three, you can take off a checker from the 6 point and a checker from the 3 point. If you have no checkers on the points indicated by your dice, you must make a move using a checker from a higher point. Whenever possible, a player must move a checker. But you do not have to bear off as long as you can make another legal move. If one of your checkers is hit during the bearing off, it goes back to the bar and you must then bring that checker back into play from the start. You cannot continue to bear off until that checker is back on your home board.

## The Doubling Cube

Backgammon is played for a mutually agreed stake per point. Each game will start at one point. A doubling cube is used to keep track of the stakes. There are six numbers on the cube: 2, 4, 8, 16, 32, 64 – hence the name, doubling.

At any time in the game, a player can offer to double the stakes. He must do this before he rolls his dice. His opponent can either accept or decline. If he accepts, the game continues at the doubled stake. If he refuses the double, he concedes the game and one point. Once a double has been accepted, that player 'owns' the cube and can use it to make the next double.

# PLAYING THE GAME

# PLAYING
# THE GAME

OK, your ten minutes are up. If you have been concentrating hard you should be ready to play your first game. All you need now is someone to play with. If they can't play, you can show off and teach them; if they can, ask them to be gentle with you. There's still a lot to learn, and most of it is in a thicker book than this one. But here are some tips and tricks that will help you on your way.

## Beaver

If you are doubled, you may immediately redouble and still retain the cube. This is called a 'beaver'. Your opponent can either accept or refuse as with a normal double. The beaver is an optional extra. Before starting a game players can decide whether or not to use it.

## Count Your Pips

You are White and Black offers a double. Will you accept or reject the offer? Is it an offer you can't refuse? Whatever it is, your decision must be based on hard facts. A quick look at the relative positions will not be enough, you will need to do a pip count. This will tell you exactly the number of pips (dots on the dice) required to get home.

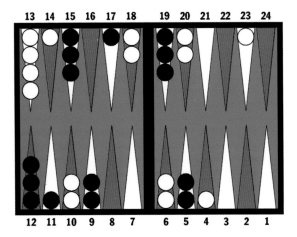

On the board on the previous page, you have one checker on the 23 point and two checkers on the 20 point. That makes 23 plus 2 x 20, which equals 63. Let's add up the rest from the 18 point: that's 36 + 14 + 52 + 20 + 12 + 4 = 138 plus the 63. Now you know you have 201 pips, but what about Black?

For Black you need to do the same thing by inverting the numbers. The two checkers on the 5 point are on the 20 point, that's 40 pips. Then continuing around the board, Black has 32 + 14 + 39 + 30 + 8 + 18 = 141, plus the 40 = 181. This means you need to roll 201 and Black only needs 181.

Although you both have three checkers in your home boards, and what appears at a glance to be an even board, White will need to roll 20 more pips in a race to finish. On top of that, your opponent gets to throw first. Black could just throw a two and a one, and you might throw double sixes – suddenly you're one pip ahead. The question is: do you feel lucky? Whatever happens, counting pips saves money.

## Primes

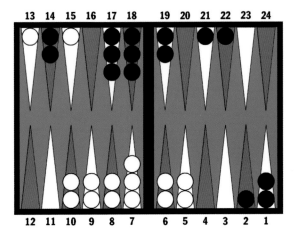

This a very strong position for White. White has built up a six-point prime: six points (10, 9, 8, 7, 6, 5) with two checkers or more on each. Black will not be able to escape. A six-point prime gives you time to move your other checkers around the board while your opponent can't get out. They are a prime piece of real estate. Build them well and look after them.

Try to stop your opponent from building primes by moving your checkers out of your opponent's home board early. You will need to take some risks by exposing your checkers.

## Duplication

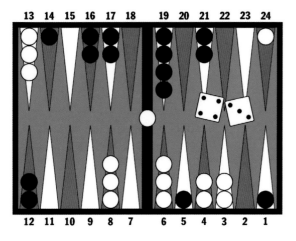

In the example shown above, White has thrown a
four and a three and has to enter the board with
the three on 22. The four needs to be played
wisely. 13/9 will allow Black any four for a hit.
Black also needs a four to build on White's 5
point. This is called 'duplication'.

If White plays 8/4, it is a conservative move. But if he plays 24/20, it gives Black a chance to roll either fives, threes or ones to hit and fours to make the 20 point. Limiting your opponent's choices forms an important part of your backgammon skills. Think hard about your options. Getting off the bar is only one important move you should make.

At this level, backgammon can be complicated, but good players try to make the game complicated for their opponents.

## Gammons and Backgammons

At the end of a game, if the losing player has borne off at least one checker, he only loses the amount shown on the doubling cube, in this case 8.

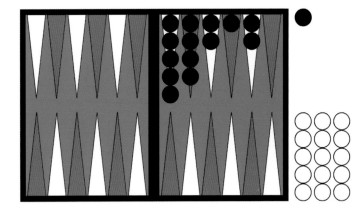

If nobody has doubled, he will lose only one point. If he has not got any of his checkers off the board, he is 'gammoned'. He then loses twice the amount on the doubling cube.

Here Black is gammoned.

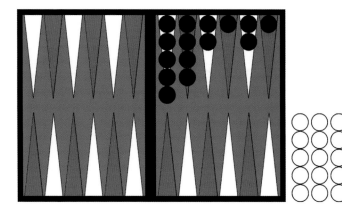

Even worse, and the ultimate catastrophe, is if he still has a checker on the bar or in the winning player's home board – he is then 'backgammoned' and will lose three times the amount on the doubling cube.

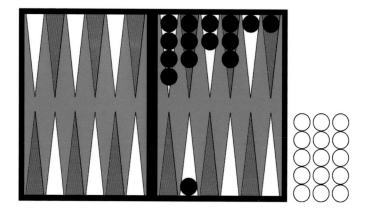

Disaster – Black is backgammoned!

## The Jacoby Rule

Under this rule, a gammon and a backgammon
(see page 40) will only count for double or triple
the number on the doubling cube if the cube has
been offered and accepted. This encourages a
player with a good lead to offer the cube, possibly
ending the game early if his opponent declines
and thus speeding up the play.

## Automatic Doubles

If both players throw identical numbers on the first
roll, the stakes are doubled. The doubling cube is
placed in the middle of the board and turned to 2.

## Good Players

Throughout the game, top players will 'study' the board. Their eyes will always be focused on the changing positions of the checkers. They are continually assessing and dissecting the ebb and flow of the game. Each game will always have a story to tell. The only time their eyes leave the board is when they look you in the eye as they offer you the doubling cube. A game can change in seconds, so try not to blink.

## Luck versus Skill

Backgammon is a wonderful game because, win or lose, you can hold your head up high. If you win you can claim it was skill, and if you lose you can say it was bad luck.

Although a lucky roll of the dice can change a game, superior skill will always win the day.

Whatever happens, you will have a lot of fun. But be warned, backgammon can be very addictive. You'll find yourself playing when you should be doing other things.

There are Internet sites and servers where you
can play people all over the world.

Luckily, a backgammon board comes in a handy carrying case, accepted by all major airlines as hand baggage. Take it on holiday; it will always provide some entertainment on the beach or on a terrace with an evening drink.

## Double Trouble?

Knowing when to use or accept the doubling cube comes with experience. As a beginner you can play your games and never use it at all. Both players can decide not to use it. As you improve, you find it adds to the excitement and skill of the game. It certainly will make you think. Just remember, you don't automatically have to use it when you are ahead, and you don't have to refuse it when you are behind.

'Owning' the cube is a big advantage. And as most games can change dramatically with a few rolls of the dice, all is not won or lost until the checkers have left the building. Top players can calculate the odds and most positions. So, just like bookmakers, they usually win. Remember, either player can offer the doubling cube on his turn before rolling the dice, but once it has been accepted for the first time, that player owns it.

# ENDING THE GAME

Ending the game in a decisive way is yet another skill to be learned. But as you must be aware by now, backgammon is a game that combines both luck and skill, but not necessarily in that order.

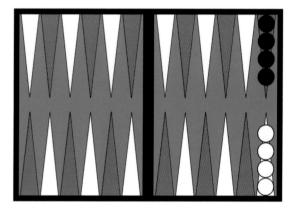

In the situation shown left, any throw will get two checkers off the board. Any roll of doubles will finish the game. But who goes first?

If White rolls first and Black doesn't throw a double on the first throw, White wins.

If Black rolls first and White doesn't throw a double on the first throw, Black wins.

There is a 1 in 6 chance of throwing a double. It could be your lucky day.

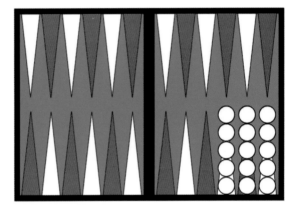

If your home board looks like this, you'll have no problems finishing off.

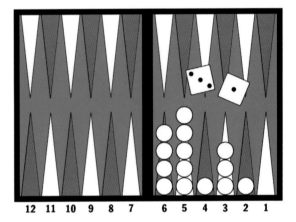

The trouble is that at some stage most home boards look like this. You throw a three and a one. What do you do? You can bear off with the three, but not with the one; you will have to move. What do you do? It's always good to reduce a pile of checkers, so 5 to 4 is a good move. Try not to leave gaps and don't let checkers pile up.

Like all addictive games, such as chess, bridge and poker, backgammon gets more complex when played at the highest level. Good players are like astrophysicists; their brains can assemble, dissect and calculate in nanoseconds. They can be quite scary, but don't worry. Just make sure you are not playing for money you can't afford to lose. You'll be the winner in the end.

So grab your board and start playing. Good luck!

# Glossary

**ANCHOR** A point in your opponent's home board or their bar point, occupied by two or more of your checkers.

**BACKGAME** When you have two or more anchors in your opponent's home board waiting to hit as he brings his checkers into his board.

**BACKGAMMON** When your opponent has one or more checkers in your home board or on the bar and has not managed to bear off at least one checker. You win three times the value of the doubling cube.

**BAR** The line that separates the two halves of the board, where hit checkers are placed.

**BAR POINT** A player's 7 point.

**BEAR OFF** To take checkers off your home board.

**BEAVER** Accepting an offer of the doubling cube and redoubling while retaining 'ownership' on your side of the board.

**BLOT** A single checker occupying a point.

**BLITZ** A concentrated attack or bombardment of your opponent's checkers with the sole objective of sending them back onto the bar.

**BROKEN PRIME** A prime with a gap in it.

**DOUBLE** A roll where both dice show the same number. Also an offer of the doubling cube.

**DUPLICATION** A way of reducing the number of good rolls available to your opponent (see page 38).

**GAMMON** When your opponent has not managed to bear off any checkers, but has no checkers in your home board or on the bar. You win twice the value of the doubling cube.

**GOLDEN ANCHOR** Your 20 point and your opponent's 5 point.

**HIT** To land one of your checkers onto a point occupied by only one of your opponent's checkers, sending it back to the bar.

**MID POINT** A player's 13 point.

**PIP COUNT** The number of pips you need to roll to get all your checkers into your home board and bear them off.

**PRIME** At least four or more consecutive points occupied by two or more checkers of the same colour.

**RACE** When a game is past the hitting stage and becomes a straight race to the finish.

**SLOT** To place a blot on a strategic point with the aim of blocking that point if your checker is not hit.

**TAKE** To accept the offered doubling cube.